THE RIGHT WAY

RULES FOR LIVING & WINNING

ANSHUMAN SHARMA

Dedicated to Sonu & Guddan

Contents

Preface   *ix*

  1. # 1: Never Ever Give Up   1

  2. # 2: Be A King In Your Domain   3

  3. # 3: Leave Your Comfort Zone Behind   5

  4. # 4: Be Ready To Sacrifice   7

  5. # 5: Think Deep And Work Hard To Achieve   9
     Something Of Importance In Life

  6. # 6: Strive For Excellence   11

  7. # 7: Build And Maintain Good Human Relations   13

  8. # 8: Do It Now   15

  9. # 9: Work Hard, Smartly   17

10. # 10: Be Fast, But Maintain Quality   19

11. # 11: Proud Decreases You   21

12. # 12: Failure As An Advantage   23

13. # 13: Be Crystal Clear In Everything   25

14. # 14: Results Are Superior To Words   27

15. # 15: Enjoy Whatever You Do   29

16. # 16: The Best Story Should Move With You   31

17. # 17: Never Share Your Problems   33

18. # 18: Complaining Nature Is Bad   35

19. # 19: Control Emotions, To Be Rational   37

20. # 20: Keep Your Mind Calm And At Peace With   39
     Itself

21. # 21: Take The Conscious Control Of Your   41

Contents

Decisions And Actions

22. # 22: To Be Done – Get It Done   43

23. # 23: Miracle Do Not Happen, You Need To Make Them Happen   45

24. # 24: Set Deadlines For Completing Work   47

25. # 25: Have Faith On Something   49

26. # 26: Self-belief Is The Driving Force   51

27. # 27: Will Power   53

28. # 28: Enjoy The Journey   55

29. # 29: Always Be Enthusiastic And Lively   57

30. # 30: Be Fit And Healthy   59

31. # 31: Give Wings To Your Creativity   61

32. # 32: Daily Activities, Tasks, And Results   63

33. # 33: Control The Environment Instead Of Environment Controlling You   65

34. # 34: Passion For Something   67

35. # 35: Speak Less But Whenever Speak, Speak Gold   69

36. # 36: Improve Daily   71

37. # 37: Maximum Productivity From Time   73

38. # 38: Consider Your Body Like A Place Of Worship   75

39. # 39: Do Not Demand But Command Respect   77

40. # 40: Kill Negativity Immediately   79

Contents

41. # 41: Never Be Complacent — 81

42. # 42: Every Activity Needs Best Planning & Implementation — 83

43. # 43: Your Touch Should Make Everything Gold — 85

44. # 44: Bring The Best Out Of Others — 87

45. # 45: A Person Should Feel Great With You — 89

46. # 46: Do Every Task Sincerely — 91

47. # 47: Power Of Patience Create Differentiation — 93

48. # 48: Punctuality — 95

49. # 49: Respect Your Words — 97

50. # 50: Perseverance — 99

About Author — 101

Preface

The differentiation between success and failure is based upon the way we perceive the daily events of life and the way we react or act on them. Every person has their set of problems in their lives but a winner converts them into opportunities, while a loser converts even opportunities into problems and blaming everyone else for their difficulties in life. A loser can indict the whole world for the pain in her life; in contrast a winner would enjoy everything in her life while appreciating her life and getting value out of it. Losers are generally confused fellows who lack focus and commitment for anything. In contrast, the winners have clarity about everything in their lives. They are optimistic people who look for possibilities in their lives. The basic difference between a winner or a loser is the foundations on which her life is built.

Foundations are the values and beliefs of a person, which are strictly followed by the people in their life. Foundations define the life of the person, the way she lives and the decisions she takes in her life. They bring the clarity in the life of the person by helping her to embrace the right choices from the options presented to her. A person with clarity generally has a set of personal principles or rules based upon which she lives her life. These principles define her actions in life, making her to commit for something while rejecting others. The clarity arising out of foundations improves her focus on actions, making them more efficient and effective.

Not all foundations are right and help in getting success in life, instead they pull us down. These foundations are built on wrong beliefs and values. Some people are wrong in saying that these values are context based, as they serve a group of people while it may have negative effect on others. According to them, these values must be considered as right as they are helpful for a group of people, at least. But the definition of right evolves from the general principles of morality which outlines the equality, happiness and prosperity of all human being irrespective of their association.

We all may have our set of beliefs and values which are learnt and experienced over a long period of time, repeatedly, throughout our lifetime. They are responsible, as they define our decisions and actions, for the situation we are in today, which could be good or bad. Every person needs to know the right foundations which can take every person towards their goals. We need to review our foundations some of which could be wrong.

This work focuses on the foundations which are right and would take any person towards their success. These foundations would help any person to review her beliefs, principles and rules in life to make the necessary corrections. The foundations specified are used by people to bring the necessary positive changes in their lives. You can meet any successful person and identify their foundations and principles of their life, in most of the cases the foundations would be derivative of the points presented in this book.

This book is written in extremely simple format so that anyone, even a layman, is able to understand it completely. The descriptions in the book are kept minimal so that each foundation is understood in few minutes. Excessive description, examples and case studies are intentionally avoided so as to keep the book within the reasonable word limits and to deliver the message to readers with maximum value.

This book can be read in any order as the description of each foundation is mutually exclusive. Readers can start to read from point 1 or they can start for point 50 or they can start from any point in between. But, must make sure that they go through each and every point to understand the description clearly. These points should be analyzed in the context of each reader and they should be able to identify the ways to implement these foundations in their lives. It should be noted that the complacency should not be shown in its implementation and it should be immediate. The book can be taken as a guide, which can be used over a period of time by taking each foundation every day, grasping its depth. It can be experienced and utilized for the whole day so that it could also be used in future.

It is hoped that this book would unleash the hidden potential of several people all over the world by making them better, successful and would make our world a better place to live.

1: NEVER EVER GIVE UP

The basic difference between a winner and a loser is that any situation, however tough, cannot compel a winner on giving up on something, which she has in her focus. She would be clear about focusing on something which is in sync with her life goals. Her next step would be to achieve these goals. Anything below the desired outcome would be rejected and her efforts would be supported by her peak performance levels.

This foundation creates a differentiation between people who would fight back till the end and those who would leave midway. In most cases people give up near to their destination, without realizing that they are responsible for missing success in their life. A person with an attitude of 'Never Giving Up' would have much higher chances of getting success in life in comparison with a person who 'Gives Up' after trying 'Enough'.

To develop this foundation you need to know your existing attitude, its impact in your life and the reasons for you to carry it. This foundation requires commitment and passion for the work you do. You need to do something to which you can commit and enjoy the process, till you achieve the desired output. You need to build a state of mind in which either you should not initiate anything or once committed, it should be pursued till you get results.

2: BE A KING IN YOUR DOMAIN

Today's global economy is extremely competitive and you need to be really good to even survive in this environment. You must have observed successful people in your life who are outstanding in something and they keep building this excellence. With time they become virtually unbeatable in that area. You need to be indomitable in a specific area of your life to get noticed. This means that you get required output and superior results with your competency.

This foundation would make you unique and create a definite positioning about you in the minds of people. Your focus would make you consistently better in this area. For example, the best person in software environment of Java would have a special attraction in the IT market. With more experience and enhanced competency the value proposition of the person would improve consistently.

Analyze and identify the area of your interest, in which you could be best. If you do not have one, then you need to choose one, commit to it and plan to become the best in the chosen area. You should identify the area for expertise which would have significance in your future life, ambitions and personal plans. Set deadlines and take intense actions to become the best in the field with great value proposition for the market.

3: LEAVE YOUR COMFORT ZONE BEHIND

Most of us want to remain in our comfort zone for the similar reasons, which is that it provides a sense of security. But we need to understand that this is the biggest obstacle in achieving our dreams. If we are a dreamer and have big ambitions in life then we must come out of our comfort zone, as this is the only way to achieve our desired results. Taking challenges should become the part of our habit, while achieving results the part of our consistence quest. The successful results of these challenges would take us towards our goals.

Comfort zone assures a mediocre life in which a large part of our life is controlled by others. In this state the ambitions would always remain impractical as an average person would shun hard decisions and tough actions. Comfort zone is not for ambitions people as they continuously move forward, towards their goals. Ambitions of a person unleash her best performance and competency levels. Challenges and responsibilities test our limits and simultaneously make us better. It improves our confidence and enhances our firmness to achieve our goals.

We need to consciously check and decide about the challenges to be taken, prepare for them and finally accept them. These actions should be oriented towards our objectives and goals, taking us near them. Each challenge would make us better and more equipped to take more challenges and responsibilities.

4: BE READY TO SACRIFICE

It is quoted that 'nothing is free', even success follows this principle. Any success requires a lot of endeavors and sacrifices. A topper at a university spends sleepless nights to get high marks and an entrepreneur with high valuation of his company may have worked for 100 hours per week. Any success comes with sincere and repeated efforts. To achieve your goal, you need to be ready to sacrifice your sleep, luxury, entertainment, comfort and even earning.

This foundation is important as it makes a person ready to pay the required cost to get the success, whether it is hard-work, less time for self or tough environment. They need to understand that the success would not be free, instead they would move slowly towards it with their will-power and commitment.

You need to decide on goals based upon your ambitions. Understand the requirement to get the success in the specified goals. Develop a plan and take firm steps towards it. You must understand that future achievements would be proportional to the efforts you are ready to put and risks you would take.

5: Think Deep and Work Hard to Achieve Something of Importance in Life

How do we define achievement? It is something which has certain value for us. It means that the output of the achievements should be beneficial to us in some way. We also need to know the weight of each achievement for us, so that the efforts and resources could be allocated based upon priorities. In addition to this understanding, it is necessary to know that these results would be attained only with deep thought and hard-work, as without it nothing important can be attracted in life.

We get satisfaction with our relevant achievements. Our career and personal life depend upon these results. This foundation should make us clear that 'luck' and 'chance' would not work till we really put genuine efforts for it.

We need to accept that one of the inseparable parts of our life is the depth of thinking and hard work. It means that for any task we should think rationally and be ready to toil to get the results, if required.

6: STRIVE FOR EXCELLENCE

Work is the necessary part in every person's life, it is required for survival. The only thing which differentiates between two humans is the quest for excellence which is generally evident in the work they do. A person who is focused on quality of output would put her heart & soul to perform at her best and to get the excellence in her work. While any effort below this level would lead to mediocre results. Skills and competency to perform the task is the necessary precondition to get results and bring brilliance to it.

An individual focused on excellence would automatically gain superiority in her group as her output would certainly be better in comparison to others. Brilliance has its sheen, which is visible easily to everyone. The quality of work is great supporter of success and without it any worthwhile result cannot be achieved.

Your commitment to greatness would change everything in your life as it has the power to raise the level a person immediately. To bring quality in your work you need to be extremely serious about it and ready to put your best efforts to get the remarkable output. You should connect your satisfaction with the excellence of output, which means that without the desired output you would not get peace of mind. It would make you a value focused person for whom the basic meaning of output would be the excellence in results.

7: BUILD AND MAINTAIN GOOD HUMAN RELATIONS

Winners are extremely good at building relationships. Good human relations can be defined as the different individuals connected with mutual trust, respect and benefits. 'Mutual' is an important word here as without mutual trust any relationship cannot survive. People should work together to perform better and achieve complex targets while enjoying results together. People become well-wishers of each other and support each other in getting success.

Good human relations are essential for both personal and professional life. It gives you the sense of social connectivity, which is important for human growth. Better relations with other people give support to achieve goals and targets.

To build good relationship with other people you need to add value to them and in return, hopefully, they would add value to you. The best policy is to improve the life of people and help them get success, without expecting anything in return. With time you would be astonished by looking at the response of the people towards you.

8: DO IT NOW

Generally, people are in the habit of procrastination, which is to delay decisions and actions without genuine reasons. The delay is actually due to their weaknesses like laziness, incompetency or to fill time with nonexistent work. We can find inaction everywhere, it reduces productivity and increase costs. The solution to procrastination is result orientation with specified targets and deadlines. You need to know the required results to obtain and the time period attached to it. Deadlines define the maximum time duration during which the task must be completed. You should set the priorities for completing the tasks to get the maximum output from your time.

This foundation is linked to results. Build on this foundation to release many locked results in your life. Once you learn to tackle procrastination you immediately become an action-oriented person, who gets results. It can transform a person from a liability to an asset for her organization.

Print in big letters "Do it Now – Just Now" and put it in-front of you. Now follow it. Do not delay any task for any reason. It is said that "If you have to do a task tomorrow then do it today, and if you have to do a task today then do it now". You need to get the maximum output from your time. Set priorities for your tasks by keeping most important one on the top. Build this foundation and become a collector of results.

9: WORK HARD, SMARTLY

There is always a conflict between hard-work and smart-work for getting success. Hard work is the necessary ingredient in any type of work but for results the person needs to be smart enough to get the best output from the hard work. Some lazy people discard hard work and concentrate only on working smartly, which is nothing but to justify their habit of procrastination. In fact, the real formula is working hard, smartly, which is the basic foundation for getting desired output. So it is necessary to understand the true meaning of 'hard work' which is putting maximum efforts for a task in the smartest possible way.

For satisfactory experience, toiling for the work is necessary, as it does not leave any regret behind. This foundation opens the doors of success, as it creates an extremely powerful force to crack any hindrances on the path. It builds confidence and gives enthusiasm to the person who believes that she is putting her best efforts. This foundation improves you every day.

This foundation is built on logic, focus, common-sense and emotions. To work smartly you need to look at the task rationally and use logic and fundamentals to get the maximum productivity from it. You can use latest tools and technologies to improve your performance and can learn from other successful executions. Emotions are required to put your maximum efforts to the task, making you perform at your peak. To achieve results, you should connect to the task and consciously compel yourself to put your best in the work you are doing. You need to consider your work, professional or personal, as one of the most important part of your life and do it passionately.

10: BE FAST, BUT MAINTAIN QUALITY

The speed of doing the task is important in defining an individual's productivity. The productivity of an operation allows a person to complete more than normal, which is good for both professional and personal life. But it is essential to understand that the speed of performing any task should not be at the cost of quality of the output. Work is extremely flexible and it fills all the time allocated to it. If five hours are allotted to the task of one hour, then this task would fill five hours completely, to get completed. This understanding gives us an important insight about knowing the task and allocating right time to it.

This foundation simply makes you more productive, you are able to perform more tasks in same amount of time. It will improve your effectiveness and your earnings. Higher productivity brings in more work satisfaction and rewards, which leads to increased interest in work.

Following steps are required to build this foundation:

- Train and equip yourself well to perform the required tasks effectively.
- Remain extremely sincere for the task
- Know the time required to complete the task
- Perform at your peak without compromising on quality of the output

11: PROUD DECREASES YOU

The biggest intoxication for human beings is from the influence of money and power as they control the mind completely. This intoxication weakens any rationality for decisions and actions. People tend to judge others based upon their status and positions instead of their character and knowledge. Superiority complex influences the behavior which guides the people's decisions. People start to feel proud of their identity which impacts their personality and actions. This type of feeling is damaging for the person and other people connected to her. This can be considered as 'negative proud'.

There is one more category of proud which makes a person enthusiastic and adds value to everyone. This can come from teamwork and hard-work. It never raises any type of negative emotions, instead makes a person energetic to perform better. This is a type of energy which adds value to everyone and increase happiness for all. This is considered as 'constructive proud'. People can be proud for their Country, University, Community or School. Constructive proud never affects people in negative way instead adds value to everyone.

Negative proud is unscrupulous, as its sole purpose is to project self-superiority over others. It spoils relationships and hurts other's self-respect. A person with proud has low self-esteem and has weakness in character. It builds guilt and people tend to regret the decisions and actions under the influence of proud. You need to be repulsive to negative proud arising from any source. It is important to understand that a person with high self-esteem would not have any feeling of proud.

To build this foundation you need to first be able to recognize and differentiate between the constructive and negative proud. If you consider someone else as inferior then you can clearly categorize the dominance of negative feelings. You should consider the money, power and success to you as gift to help and support others to make them successful. The value proposition of proud is nil instead it become an addition to the list of weaknesses.

12: FAILURE AS AN ADVANTAGE

Challenges and problems are the part of life. We can either accept them with open hands or yelp about it. The former is better as the attitude of accepting problems makes them your supporter in growth. If you could learn from each experience and grow with them then every challenge and problem becomes your teacher. The problems in your work life would make your relations stronger and the challenges in your personal life would make you a better manager and entrepreneur.

Some people blame luck for the tough events in their life. They consider those as insolvable problems instead of considering life challenges as the opportunity to improve themselves. These events drive a person to work at their peak potential to create value from the problems. If managed properly these events would bring out the best by shaking you out of your complacency.

To become a transformed person who gets success through her optimism a minor change in the perception is required which should help you to look at every event in life as an opportunity to become a better and stronger person. Once you consider these challenges as a normal part of your life then you become rational in your approach by making yourself emotionally detached from them. You need to look logically for solutions and the course of action to get desired results. You need to take decisions followed by firm actions. Your final objective is to come out of these events better and stronger than before.

13: BE CRYSTAL CLEAR IN EVERYTHING

A happy person is a clear person who knows what she wants in life and the actions she needs to take to achieve those. Clarity brings decisiveness which leads to the intensity in action. It means the person knows the direction in which she needs to move. She is at peace with herself and doesn't need any approvals from anybody to take required decisions. She has high self-esteem and acts as leader to others who need direction in life and clarity at work. Clarity builds good relations and attracts respect.

The importance of clarity is evident from the fact that all right things are performed by individuals who know 'what they are doing?' It is important in life for being decisive about actions. It makes a person dynamic by making her action more results oriented. Being clear about self and environment makes life simpler for the people who want to get success in life.

Clarity is also directly related to rationality as a clear decision and action has to be rational. An irrational decision is generally the product of a confused mind. Any decision or action should be supported by logical reasoning and clear objectives. It is to be noted that every time or in every case we cannot have the luxury of complete information for getting required clarity to take firm decisions. In these events we take decisions based upon some assumptions, though each assumption should have logical reasoning. These decisions are to be followed until the assumptions are proven to be completely wrong. For clarity in decisions and firmness in actions it is required that the person have the complete understanding about self. This means that introspection is required on regular basis which reveals the strengths and weaknesses of a person. Any issue should be analyzed deeply with all the facts, information, assumptions, reasons etc. You need to analyze it, feel it intuitively to get complete clarity about it. Take your decisions based upon this clarity.

14: RESULTS ARE SUPERIOR TO WORDS

Any action should be taken with the focus on results, as they are the only reason for which the action was initiated. The emphasis on results is generally accompanied with deadlines in which the specific time limit is decided to get the required results. Many times, people initiate a task without the end in sight, which means that they lack clarity about the results to be achieved. It defeats their purpose of putting efforts to the task. The confusion about the definition of output would itself weaken any plan and action to achieve it.

This foundation is important in improving the focus of the person on the real aspect of the task. It would help in preparing better for the execution of the task. This focus would also improve the planning for the task and helps in taking the right decisions. Achieved results for any activity shows the genuineness of the efforts put to it, as any apathy to the task would affect the output. Results are the best test for a person to evaluate her skills, competencies and genuineness of the efforts. Results are also the best teacher as, if used sincerely, they points to your faults and motivate you to improve your future results.

To build this foundation you need to be serious about your results, which would immediately have the positive impact on your efforts. For every task you need to know the output you want and the way to achieve the required results. You should accept it honestly that the most important part of any task is its output, which needs to be right. In many cases you would need to iterate the action for getting the proper output. The complete set of activities for every task should be taken as a learning experience while enjoying every moment of the process.

15: ENJOY WHATEVER YOU DO

Many times, we are stuck with things and activities which are disliked by us, and it affects us mentally and physically. This deteriorates our performance at work and hurts our confidence. The people who are excellent in their work and consistently produce great results are the people who like their work. These people act like intrapreneurs i.e. they act like entrepreneurs inside their organizations. This rule is valid in the life too, a marriage breaks down only when the married couple feels pain with each other, and they do not enjoy each other's company. The rule is simple 'Do what you like and like what you do'.

This foundation is fundamental to living our life that we should enjoy our life and all of its phases. This has a simple meaning that whatever the condition in life we need to live it to fullest and find ways to make it better, every single day.

Sometimes, we will not be able to get everything of our choice, then, we should follow the other part of the rule that 'we should like whatever we do'. This does not mean that we need to get stuck to it, instead we should try our best to be in the domain of our interest, but if that is not possible then we should perform in the task in hand with complete sincerity. We can find interesting ways to like the task, for example, we can find new ways to be more productive in it or improve the quality of output, without increasing cost or efforts substantially.

To build this foundation we need to have a purpose in our life, which defines the objective of our existence. Our goals and objectives can be stated with the help of this purpose of life. We should get involved in the activities which are liked by us and has some specific meaning for us. Even if we are imposed with the tasks which are despised by us, we should give it complete sincerity by putting our best efforts to it. If we cannot do that then we should reject the activity entirely.

16: THE BEST STORY SHOULD MOVE WITH YOU

You should become the hero in your life story. The basic idea behind this foundation is that you make your life interesting, without any hitch or hesitation. For example, if you are excited about a specific movie which is full of interesting events and the lead actor meets a lot of people but the focus of the movie is always on the lead actor, as he is supposed to carry out the most interesting events. Similarly, you should also try to be the hero of your life and you should choose to keep the story most interesting. This attitude would make our life interesting.

With this foundation we chose to become happier and satisfied in our life. We realize that this power was always with us, but now we have chosen to utilize it. This thinking immediately fills our life with excitement as if we become the main character in the story of our life and interestingly, we are also the writer of this story. To keep it interesting we need to initiate a lot of things and put required efforts to get success. It helps in changing the perception of our life to positive. It also makes us the writer of our destiny.

It is necessary to understand that the design of our life is in our hands and this is a choice we always have. If we have a boring life then we have chosen it, while all satisfied people have chosen to live a happy life. Once we become the writer and the main character of our life story, which should be interesting with adventures and success, we tend to make our life better.

17: NEVER SHARE YOUR PROBLEMS

Every human has her own set of problems in life. For each person her problems look the biggest and toughest. They want to share it with others to get sympathy, solutions, help or any type of support. They would present the pains in their life with dramatic effects and emotional outbursts. The only value of this presentation is some sort of emotional satisfaction which comes with sharing of their problems. But, the fact remains simple, no one likes a person who talks about self and wails about her life. At best, people endure these types of people and want to avoid them. This type of people attracts attention for all wrong reasons. People shun them and at most pity them and in rare case provide some marginal support to them. Some opportunists even use the information provided to them for their own benefit.

This foundation focuses on bringing the control of your life back to you. Once you become the master of your life all the problems and complexities loose strength. Your confidence level rises, weaknesses weaken and strengths build up, you feel ready to take any challenge in life.

The right way to deal with your problems in life is to deal with them yourself, as you are the only person who understands them and can solve them. You remain in control of the situation and also learn in the process, which makes you more equipped in life. When you criticize your life, it hurts your self-respect severely. It weakens the self-confidence which pulls the person further down in life. Once you decide to deal with your problems yourself, the body and mind get ready to deal with the situations. This decision brings the control back to you in your life. As the best person who would care for you is 'you', therefore, all the required solutions and actions must come from you to solve all the problems, obstructions and complexities of life. Consider difficulties as a part of life and never let your problems affect your goals and success.

18: COMPLAINING NATURE IS BAD

Each person has her set of failures which can be due to various reasons. Some people fail due to lack in competency or due to mistake of others or due to conditions which cannot be controlled. But, the most important part of any failure is the way you deal with it. You can either choose to blame yourself and regret for it or you can blame someone else for your failure to get temporary emotional satisfaction or you can minimize the damage and learn from it. Natural instinct forces us to choose either of first two while the best option requires conscious efforts.

Generally, for any failure people either blame themselves or someone else; in fact most of the people try to shift the blame to other person. This attitude is damaging for the character and morally weakens a person. People want to complain and blame someone for the problems in their life, hoping to get some help, sympathy or emotional satisfaction. A person with complaints never provides solutions, instead finds fault in anything and everything. This individual is never liked by any person and can never connect with anyone. Complaining nature damages the reputation and the personality of a person.

To build on this foundation we need to focus on few points. First, we need to put our best efforts to the work we do. Second, for any failure we should not blame anyone, including ourselves as we had put genuine efforts for it. And lastly, we should learn from our failures so that the mistakes leading to it are never repeated. We can choose to find value in everything we do in our daily lives.

19: CONTROL EMOTIONS, TO BE RATIONAL

Emotions are the natural part of every human being and they make us happy and enthusiastic, they also make us sad and despondent. Emotions can sometimes be extremely strong that they control our behavior. One of the important aspect of emotions is their influence over our decisions, which directly affects our actions. Strong emotions like love, hate and anger cloud our mind and skew our decisions, which may not be right. Our decisions and actions need to be rational which are not biased, in any way, by our emotions and feelings.

It is necessary to understand that any biased decision would not be right as it would have weak fundamentals and may not have moral grounds. The actions based upon these decisions would not be logical and can never support a person in getting success. It becomes extremely important for us to keep emotions in control while taking any decisions or action, which should not be influenced in anyway.

To build this foundation a person needs to remain conscious to this principle in which the decisions remain independent and never get influenced by your feelings about the issue. This is like the President of a country needs to remain neutral to every issue and should take decisions based upon rationality, not based upon his emotional bias for an issue. Similarly, your emotions need to be controlled and they should not affect your decision in any way.

20: KEEP YOUR MIND CALM AND AT PEACE WITH ITSELF

The daily challenges of life put a lot of pressure on mind & body and create stress and tension. These complexities can be at work-place or in people's personal lives. It affects people by diminishing their performance at work. The stress is harmful for the health of the person and is responsible for several diseases. The present lifestyle of the modern human beings of our world makes stress a part of almost everybody's life. Stress sucks joy out of the life of the person and fills it with pain and restlessness. It becomes like a vicious circle in which more stress impacts health and performance which adds intensity to stress. This cycle must be broken and the best way to do it is to ensure that the mind remains calm, without any noise of irrelevance. A tranquil mind is most efficient and can perform at high level.

A person at peace with self is likely to have a higher functioning brain than a normal person. It gives clarity of objectives and specifies required actions for getting output. Any stress in mind vanishes with calm mind and problems are tackled more objectively. Mental tension loses its strength and its causes are managed firmly so as to resolve them. Controlled mind is good for human productivity and it makes people more efficient. It makes people to think with clearness about issues which help them to take better decisions. The mind, which is free of confusion, is more optimistic about life and fills the heart with enthusiasm.

To build this foundation you need to have the control on your mind. Market is full of suggestions and information about mind-control but the best and simplest method is meditation. This is the most powerful way to have the required peace of mind. Meditation involves clearing the mind with all thoughts and making it hollow, with no ideas or thinking. This process should be repeated every day for minimum five minutes. This would have the magical effects on the practicing person, making you a better and clear thinker. The other change which is required is to be in control of everything in life, which would make you to take any decision or action with judiciousness. The person needs to be satisfied in life and needs to feel content with her achievements. This does not mean that this person is not ambitious; instead she enjoys everything in her life and has a clear focus on her goals which she achieves in the most prudent way. Finally, the person needs to believe in herself and have faith that she would get success in life.

21: Take the Conscious Control of Your Decisions and Actions

The life of a person is designed by the decisions and actions she takes in her life. Many times, these decisions and actions are taken in haste or without thoughtful considerations, which may have consequences that can last a lifetime. Any wrong decision may turn the course of life. Many people live the life with regret and guilt and they keep blaming the wrong turn of their life. If you can take the complete control of your decisions then they would be taken with complete rationality, which would depend upon the available information at that point of time.

This foundation is the part of mission to take back the control of your destiny from others. A person takes a wrong decision or action from an emotional outburst which generally arises from others actions. Once you decide to manage it, the strength of other people loosens on you, and the control comes back to you. The person becomes more responsible in taking decisions and her actions become better, effective and more productive. This new and massive responsibility creates a positive pressure to improve which makes a person more competent and skillful.

This foundation would help by giving control of your life to you by making you more responsible for your decisions and subsequent actions. The life of a person is defined by her decisions in life. Once she takes the complete responsibility for her life it transforms her into a more mature and responsible person. This also gives a feeling of freedom and control to design a desirable life, making the person more dynamic in taking actions. She takes all her decisions in the best possible way with complete research and in-depth thinking. As she understands that the delay in any decision would blunt its impact, therefore, she becomes vibrant and effective. The person also needs to be flexible and not rigid in her approach of moving forward.

22: TO BE DONE – GET IT DONE

This foundation focuses on

- Clarity of the task to be completed and
- Taking the required steps to successfully finish it

This is fairly a simple process which focuses on getting the right results in your work and in your life.

Once you are able to build this foundation then you become absolutely unstoppable as you build momentum through getting results consistently. You decide on the tasks to be done and then get them completed. This cycle becomes an unending process which keeps churning out successful results, making the person a winner. All successful people have a strong foundation in this principle.

To build this foundation you need to practice for using this principle in your life. Start using this in small activities and then move on to do bigger tasks with this principle. Your objective should be to integrate this principle into your daily life.

23: MIRACLE DO NOT HAPPEN, YOU NEED TO MAKE THEM HAPPEN

Every person has her set of challenges in living her life. It depends upon each individual to perceive these events in their own way. Some people consider fate as the defining factor in their life, for them all successful people are lucky while unlucky people cannot rise in life. According to these people success comes with miracles in life and without them a person cannot be a winner. It is true that to get success extraordinary achievements should build the path to dreams, but it is wrong to assume that these miracles happen by themselves or some external force is gifting them to winners.

Miracles do not happen by themselves, you need to make them happen.

Miracles push the life to higher level by moving them towards success. Miracles are a set of accomplishments which gives pleasure, reduces pain and takes them towards their goals in life. But the achievements need to be big to be considered as miracles. Many smaller successes could create a big triumph which could act as a miracle in life.

To create miracles in life they first need to be accepted as results, which would depend upon the commitment and execution of the person. This means every person controls the miracles in their life. To create these miracles in life a person needs to be aware about her strengths and weaknesses. She has to think big and set high but reasonable goals. Her commitment to the goal would make her perform at her peak. It is necessary to be passionate about the results and perseverance in the face of difficulties. Following these basic rules, the person can become the manager of the miracles in her life.

24: SET DEADLINES FOR COMPLETING WORK

Deadline is the time limit set to complete a specified task. Putting this limit organizes every activity in the mind of the person who performs the task with the focus on the time allocated to it. The best way to complete the task in specified time limit is to break it down into several smaller deadlines to complete the task in several steps. Deadlines are the most effective tool for the managers to get work done from the team productively. Setting the deadlines is also important in organizing and ensuring the completion of the project.

Defining the targets for a project is the right way to finish the task within time. It helps with better organization and planning to get things completed within cost and allocated duration. Deadline is a tool which is being used by doers to be an action-oriented person.

To build this foundation you need to get into the habit of setting and meeting deadlines for your tasks. These deadlines need to be logical and sincere, which means that these should not be either too tight or too light. The deadlines should be optimum, leading to completion of task in best possible way. These deadlines should make you more productive and efficient.

25: HAVE FAITH ON SOMETHING

Most of the humanity believes on some higher power which they call God and the percentage of atheist is extremely less in comparison to believers. Some people do not believe in God but have faith on some sort of intelligent energy while several people just have faith that wrong will not happen with them if they do right. Whatever it may be, faith is a powerful force, which adds to the strength & positivity of an individual. A confident and successful individual may have the trust on her skills, competencies and abilities, without finding any sense in the concept of higher power. It depends upon an individual to identify the various means which would have the positive impact in her life.

Every person needs to connect with a force in her life, which could provide with the infinite stream of positivity. A person with perseverance has faith on something, which drives her to action, even in the face of difficulties. Faith is helpful in managing stress and reducing daily pressures of life and work. It provides hope & optimism and supports people with positive perception of events. Faith is important to create miracles in life.

To get success in life the person needs to discover and connect strongly with her faith. It is important to understand that the faith can never be a weak connection with something, it needs to be genuine and unbreakable. A strong faith survives the test of time, which means that during tough times the faith become stronger by proving a strong foundation to pass through it.

26: SELF-BELIEF IS THE DRIVING FORCE

Belief is one of the most powerful constituents of human beings. Belief can be for a cause or it can be for a person, belief can be for some higher power or it can be for a purpose. All of these beliefs are extremely powerful but they all are connected to the belief on self, without which all other beliefs lose their strength. Self-belief is the trust on self to be able to perform seemingly impossible tasks. It becomes the driving force for the decisions of individual's life and provides necessary energy to take required actions. The lack of self-belief leads to low self-esteem which makes a person dependent on others to get approvals for moving ahead in life. The weakness in self-belief affects the performance of a person which directly affects her results and confidence. It is important to never underestimate the effect of self-belief in the life of a human being.

If a person has belief on herself, she becomes virtually unstoppable. It gives her an unbound confidence to take challenges and completes them successfully. She would take initiations of the tasks which are considered complex for a normal human being. People tend to take more responsibilities and perform tasks with dedication. This foundation is fundamental for building superior personalities in human beings.

To build this foundation few simple rules need to be followed:

- Become a learner and learn fast from your mistakes, the mistakes should never be repeated,
- Build new skills and competencies and they should be used in daily tasks so as to get mastery in them,
- Focus initially on small successes to build confidence, these small successes are not the milestones but act as the necessary fuel to gain momentum,
- Improve your planning and strategizing which should be practical and result focused. These strategies and plans should be flexible enough to improve with time.
- Be great at execution and implementation of plans. Execution is the most important weapon of a doer, who focuses on results,

Difficulties separate the winner from a loser. A loser quits while a winner perseveres.

27: WILL POWER

Will power is the topic which is most commonly commented but not clearly understood by people. They generally use it casually, without understanding its true value or meaning. Will power is the foundation to all motivations, without which the momentum for any task cannot be sustained. Will power is also the foundation to all commitments and dedications. Will power is the internal strength which provides the necessary driving force for any action. A powerful Will would make sure that the logical end of any task is reached even if it is full of numerous problems and hindrances.

Any go-getter has sufficient amount of Will power which provides required energy and motivation to execute the task in hand. Most of the people may initiate any task, but few would be able to carry it to the required point for getting results, in face of unwanted resistance. We must have observed people with supreme confidence in themselves who are ready to take any challenge posed to them. They are result oriented people who never stop midway. It can easily be said that any true performer in any domain have the strength of Will power with them.

Any person can have strong Will power as they already have it with them, only they have to realize it. Every human being is standing on the same level of this power but it depends upon the conscious intention of an individual to utilize it. Will power cannot be utilized without clarity in life which comes from the purpose of life. Purpose supports in setting goals of life, which are achieved through the force provided by Will power. Clarity also provides focus on the goals which should never be diluted for any reason. Will power also comes from habit, once a person gets in the habit of utilizing her Will power she would have more ease in becoming a strong 'willed' person.

28: ENJOY THE JOURNEY

For getting happiness in life, we need to enjoy every moment of it. We need to like our personal and professional part and the daily tasks in our life. The journey of life should be enjoyed by every person. We know that the results are important and we need to focus on them, but the commitment to results should not, in any way, spoil the fun of the actions taken to achieve it. As a large part of our life is full of various types of journeys, we should make them more interesting than even achieving results.

If we do not enjoy the journey then it is difficult to get results, as output is directly related to the efforts put to achieve it. The fun involved in doing things is good for people and their health. Once you learn to enjoy every expedition of life then success comes to you in the form of achievements. The enthusiasm attached to doing work makes a person an asset for the team.

To build this foundation you should be working in the area of interest, something which excites you. The liking of the task is essential in building the necessary motivation to move forward. It is also important to have patience, as the journey can be long and full of hindrances. A conscious effort would be required to gain the required energy to move forward. The journey to achieve results should be a learning experience by making the person better in the process. You should also focus on getting successful results as it helps in getting the required enthusiasm for next tasks.

29: ALWAYS BE ENTHUSIASTIC AND LIVELY

One of the keys to happy life is 'enjoying the things we do or doing things we enjoy'. The common factor in both cases is enjoying what we do which leads to happiness in life. This means we control our happiness and it is up to us to make us happy or sad. We can decide to enjoy every activity in our life and find value in them. The best way to judge the interest for a specific action or task is to understand the enthusiasm for it. You need to feel lively while doing it.

People do get stuck in activities which they do not enjoy and need to push themselves every time for action. They can never excel in that area, which would restrict them to mediocre level, restricting success from their lives. This point simply means that if we are enthusiastic about our work then success is ensured. Enthusiasm brings the best out of us making us more productive and effective in the actions we take. It is also contagious and flows from one person to another, creating a chain reaction. For example, one enthusiastic person in an office can make everyone else excited about the work they do.

A life without enthusiasm is a life not well-lived, as large part of our potential remains unutilized and we miss out on success which we could have achieved. The first rule of bringing enthusiasm in life is to be true to yourself. You need to know what would make you happy and fulfilled. There is a big difference between what 'looks' and what 'is', so define clearly which job, decisions or actions are true to your personality and character. Second rule emphasizes on taking action on the ideas generated by taking a step further towards action. Finally, to ensure that you keep enthusiasm in your life and work, reinvent both with time.

30: BE FIT AND HEALTHY

As individuals we have our dreams and goals and in the heat to achieve those, we tend to neglect the most important resource which is required to get success. This neglect makes this important resource a drag on our growth. Though it takes common sense to know that our physical and mental health would be a vehicle and force to reach our goals, but most people seem to undermine it. This mistake sometimes may affect health of the person making her less productive and reducing her chances to get success.

It is to be noticed that both physical and mental health are required in life as one without other have no value. A fit person can work productively for long hours. The performance of a fit person is generally higher than others. Similarly, people need to take efforts for the strength, sharpness and agility of mind which makes humans unique.

Based upon your body and stamina, design a daily fitness routine which would include physical exercises and body nourishments. It should be followed strictly. You can take support of the professionals for guidance. Our mind gain strength with new experiences and challenges. A person taking new initiations and responsibilities would have to learn and develop herself consistently, as they become the necessary part of her daily life.

31: GIVE WINGS TO YOUR CREATIVITY

Creativity is discovering solutions which could not be found without taking special efforts. A person who has understood the power of creativity can produce effective ideas and solutions. These unique ideas would make this person a successful person by presenting a clear differentiation between her and others.

A creative person has the high probability of success as her creative solutions would support her in getting desired results. Creativity would help in improving productivity, reducing cost and simplifying things. Creativity would act as an invaluable asset for getting success.

Every person can be creative, only they need to find the real need for it and should be ready to take efforts to utilize this strength. Creativity is discovering solutions which may not exist in public domain and are not known to others. These creative ideas can be incredibly simple and may look obvious once identified. It is a general understanding that a person has to be born creative and it cannot be developed. This is far from truth. All humans have similar level of creativity, only certain conditions, real or imaginary, may force an individual to think creatively. As rightly said that 'the need is the mother of all inventions', which specifies that if there is a strong need then people would find creative solutions for it.

32: DAILY ACTIVITIES, TASKS, AND RESULTS

Every person has their own definition of success. For some spending more time with family is success, others want to do something for society; some want power and lot many wants money. Whatever is the definition, success would require extensive efforts which would lead to output. A consistent set of these outputs would lead to success. For a motivated person all conditions are suitable for getting success.

If we define our daily actions then they could be divided in activities and tasks. Activities are the necessary daily acts which are required for living like shopping for groceries, cooking, exercising, watching television etc. Tasks are the actions which aim for success-oriented results. If the definition of success for a person is to become one of the most knowledgeable persons in a specific field, then her time spend in improving her knowledge in that area like reading book, talking to experts and gaining practical experience would amount to performing tasks.

Each one of us should know our definition of success and should understand the path to reach there. We need to know the actions and decisions we need to take to get the success. As the process of gaining success is a long-term process, therefore we need to take daily actions to reach towards it. Our day should be divided into proper set of activities and tasks. It is necessary to note that for many people the day is filled with only activities but no task, which falsely give them the feeling of performance to get results. It is required to make sure that the tasks fill a large part of the day, which would lead to results. It is necessary to understand that tasks would require serious actions with high performance levels, which should lead to producing desired results.

33: Control the Environment Instead of Environment Controlling You

Humanity lives in societies which consist of group of humans who give a specific personality to the society. This society in turn affects the behaviors of the individuals in it making them take specific decision, while restricting others. Over time these societies gains so much strength that they create their own environments in which the members of societies are supposed to function as if they are floating in it. Lot of strength and clarity would be required to behave and act differently by opposing its strong flow. Majority of the people in the society 'go with the flow' of the environment which guarantees the mediocre living standard. Some people refuse to accept the direction as specified by standards of society and are ready to take risks. These people are said to be 'going against the flow', in fact these are the people who give the new and fresh direction to the flow of the society, which is generally better.

The purpose of this point is not to suggest that the readers should choose to go against the flow, as it depends upon individuals to chart their own course in life. The main idea of this point is to suggest that the environment created by the society should not control you, forcing you to take specific decisions, which you may not like. One of the examples of this environment is peer pressure, which influences the actions of majority of people in a group. You need to keep yourself independent of the influence and the force exerted by the society which may not define the right direction for you. Instead, you should have independent thinking and should choose what is right for you.

34: PASSION FOR SOMETHING

A doer is differentiated by the enthusiasm she brings to a task, this enthusiasm comes from passion. A person with passion oozes out positivity, which infects every person, thereby making them more energetic. Passion ensures complete involvement of the person by making him put genuine efforts to the task. A person with passion would work at peak performance levels consistently for long hours. In right conditions passion does not decrease with time, instead increases with success. Passion is an internal resource which every human being possesses, but it depends upon the choice of the individual to utilize it.

A passionate person would have certain goals to pursue and would be interested in the results from the efforts. She would utilize all available resources to get the desired results. The best part of passion is that the person enjoys every moment of it. At work, passion is the key to satisfaction making an individual to look forward towards more work. An organization with passionate workers would be among the top in its industry as its employees would make it the leader in innovation, sales, operations and productivity. Passion also acts as a training tool for a person. A passionate person would take initiations and responsibilities and would learn new things to bridge any skills gap, making her more competent in the process.

Love for something is a prerequisite for bringing passion to the task. People who do not have the liking for a specific task can never bring the force of passion to it. So it becomes important that you should get involved in something you relish. Another way to become passionate is to set goals in life as they act as the lighthouse for taking decisions. A person without goals is like a lost person without any direction to focus. The energy of performance dissipates in unrequired actions, which arises due to lack of focus. Last point to consider is to perform at your best and focus on results as better performance leads to amazing performance and small successes leads to bigger successes.

Passion for something is important to live life happily and satisfactorily.

35: SPEAK LESS BUT WHENEVER SPEAK, SPEAK GOLD

There is so much of noise around, people speaking so many things, most of which have no value. Human being is a social animal and wants to communicate with other people. It is a natural tendency to speak to others as it gives joy and satisfaction. People speak about self, about they likes & dislikes and any other topic on earth. Most of the time these people speak just for speaking, not to add any value to anyone. For many people it is entertainment and for some it is a necessity as they need to have some specific hours of interaction with other people, to release their stress. All this leads to massive human interactions, most of which can be categorized as noise as it does not add any value to other person.

If we could understand this reality then we would try not to be part of noise instead we would respect our time and spoken words. Our words should be respected by others and our communication should have value for others. The words should come out of our mouth only after analysis and understanding the various perceptions of those words. This would give relevance to your words raising them to the level of gold, which everyone would like and would want to consume. It is better not to speak anything, instead to speaking something which has not value or meaning for anyone.

36: IMPROVE DAILY

Whatever we understand about humans and their psychology, one point is absolutely clear that the transformations do not happen in an instant. Any instant change is generally temporary, and the person returns to her previous state after some time. We can see the effects of instant change all around us, when some person commits to stop smoking instantly but after couple of days he is back with his cigarettes or a chubby person decides to start developing healthy food habits with physical exercises, which generally do not last even for few weeks. Though exceptions are everywhere with superior will power and commitment.

For humans the change happens slowly and incrementally, which means that the intensity of any bad habit is reduced slowly and consistently. This process weakens the habit with time, giving control back to the person to suppress it. Similar concept can be applied to build a good habit which is developed over time. For example, the habit of physical exercises is built overtime, starting with only five minutes initially.

To bring greatness in life we need to commit to bring incremental changes in us daily. We should be better tomorrow than we are today and should be better today that we were yesterday. If we can follow this rule sincerely then we can meet a 'better me' every day and we can estimate our growth, years from now.

37: MAXIMUM PRODUCTIVITY FROM TIME

The most important resource which each one of us has but it is consumed every minute is time. We have limited time in our life which consists of limited number of days. Everybody has their own definition of success, but to achieve it each one of us has some specific number of days and hours (though unknown to everyone) in our life. This perspective shows the urgency of utilizing our time in most productive way. As we have limited resource of time, we should make each day most productive. Time should not be spent but utilized consciously and effectively.

All successful people understand this principle early in their lives and use their time productively to get results which takes them towards their life goals. They are able to squeeze maximum results from their time which differentiates them from others. Most of the people do not understand the value of time in their lives and take it for granted. They do not understand that this resource is being wasted without giving the results you deserve.

It is important to understand the time from this perspective so that we are able to realize its value and appreciate it.

38: Consider Your Body Like a Place of Worship

You may believe in God or you may be an atheist but every person has a place of worship, it may be a church, synagogue, temple, mosque or place where you experience peace and completeness. The place of worship is a place of reverence where a person is honest with herself and free of all evils. As our body is our identity it should be our first place of worship. Every religion talks about the existence of God in every person, which indicates that our body becomes our place of worship.

We should respect our body as we respect our place of worship by treating it in similar or better way. Some people fill it with all type of harmful substances, damaging it in the process. If we do not respect our body, it is difficult to receive the respect in return from our body. A disrespected body would become weak and diseased, incapable of supporting the person in her quests.

You need to differentiate between the good and bad for your body and take actions which should ensure that you are respecting your body like a place of worship. You need to make sure by taking steps that these efforts are continuous, not temporary.

39: DO NOT DEMAND BUT COMMAND RESPECT

Society is a group of humans working together for common objectives, which are good for all the members of the society. Members of society are related to each other in various ways. Few take leadership role, some take supporting role and most of the people take the follower role. A society can exist only if people have regard for each other, which means that they care for each other. The care is generally mutual as it is important for keeping the society intact and working towards common good.

Humans want to be loved by others and desire to be respected in the society. They demand respect from others. Respect is generally reserved for those who are considered extraordinary in some specific way; they may be social leaders, business people or achievers in some areas. People also lose respect in the society if they lose the special position they enjoyed. The respect would never come from demanding it by commotion but by putting yourself into that unique position where the people would respect you. You can be an achiever in some specific area or you can show the leadership in something or you can be an inventor of something, you would need to create a niche for yourself which would be respected by the people. Once you are able to do it then you do not need to demand respect you would command respect in the society.

The unique position which we have discussed above would require hard work and dedication which keep it away from normal people. If we want to command respect in society then we should be ready to sacrifice for it by putting our full efforts for it.

40: KILL NEGATIVITY IMMEDIATELY

We are thinking animals and a large number of thoughts keep coming to our mind every minute. These could be related to our environment, home, associates or just unrelated thinking coming out of blue. As human mind is extremely powerful it would process any data or information and would develop several interpretations for it. It depends upon the individuals to choose the interpretation presented to them by the mind. Ironically, most of the people are programed to choose the negative outcomes as positive options requires efforts from the individual. We should choose the positive option and immediately kill any negative thought coming to the mind.

Killing negativity does not mean that we overlook everything but we need to be rational and strong enough to suppress any thinking which would limit our functioning. We should be cautious and intelligent enough to understand the pitfalls and potential problems but we should eradicate any negative thinking which would restrict our actions as we have to choose the best option and move forward.

We need to analyze our thinking patterns and the influence they have on our decisions. We also need to know the strength of these patterns and their impact on our actions. The rational analysis would clearly specify which negative ideas need to be immediately suppressed and which ideas should be taken as caution.

41: NEVER BE COMPLACENT

It takes a lot of efforts to get the command and control on something. Every new activity moves from initial transient state to steady state, once stabilized it can easily be performed. For example, a new sales person may have to be extremely careful in the market to interact with his clients as he needs to follow all the rules and procedures while developing business relationship with the customer. As this is a learning process for the salesperson, he may initially commit some mistakes even if he is taking all precautions. Over a period of time his experience gives ease in the job and he can perform the same activities without much efforts. This is true for most of the other occupations too, in which people get ease with experience.

In some cases, the results deteriorate with experience, which is eccentric as improvement in expertise should improve results. This main reason for these cases is complacency, which is the lack of sincerity with experience. Complacency is a common problem of humans which reduces the seriousness of effort which is being put to the action. This lack of sincerity affects the quality of results.

It is important to understand that we should not be complacent in our work and activities. The effect of complacency would be evident in the output received through our efforts.

42: EVERY ACTIVITY NEEDS BEST PLANNING & IMPLEMENTATION

Success is defined by the results we get in the activities which take us towards our goals. For this to happen we need to first know our definition of success and goals to achieve. Each goal requires a set of activities which direct our efforts towards success. The key to achievement is the getting desired results in the activities for goals.

It is to be noted that the keys to get results in the work we do are the quality of planning and strength of execution. Any weakness on the part of either planning or execution would not get us results. Planning consists of the design of the steps to be taken to achieve the goals, which is complete with various scenarios and assumptions. Execution consists of the actual action on the plan which leads to results.

Execution requires skills and competencies to get the results.

Each activity needs to be divided into two areas of planning and execution and analyzed for their effectiveness. We need to put our best resources to get the planning and execution right for each activity.

43: YOUR TOUCH SHOULD MAKE EVERYTHING GOLD

There are some people whose presence creates problems in the work we do, they reduce the overall productivity of the team. There are many whose presence has no noticeable difference in the team which means that their value addition is average and remains around the existing team members. Then there are people whose 'touch make things gold', i.e. they add extensive value with their presence. This can be measured by the difference of output with or without their presence. These people are either highly skilled or are normal people with compassion to sincerely help others. They are extremely serious about the work they undertake and put their best to achieve desired results. They always aspire to surpass every other person, even themselves, in quality, efficiency and sincerity. This passion for performance and contribution adds a unique charm in their personalities.

A person is judged by the value she adds to other person, whether it is business, politics, teaching or even in personal relations. It goes unsaid that the person needs to be moral and honest. Every human being is blessed with the ability to learn and perform. Great performers have a commitment to themselves to never take any work casually, instead they bring optimism and enthusiasm to the work they do.

If we make a commitment to ourselves and keep it forever then we can transform ourselves immediately. The commitment would be to be sincere and honest to anything we do and put our maximum force to it, while keeping our focus on results. If we can follow this commitment infallibly in our lives then amazing things would happen like we would improve ourselves and would be considered as a precious asset by all.

44: Bring the Best Out of Others

How is a leader different from others? What is that unique ability which makes him a leader? How does an organization become great? To answer these questions, we need to understand few basic points. Every person has the potential to achieve great feats in any area or domain. In most of the cases people utilize only a fraction of that potential due to various reasons. We must have observed ordinary people performing extraordinarily during difficult circumstances. The main reason of this performance is the choice they made to save themselves and their families by doing anything which is required. The sense of urgency and motivation to act drive people to put their best in the task they perform.

The leader is a person who has the ability to drive people to extraordinary performances, to which they were not even aware about themselves. A high performing team is built by the enthusiastic individuals who are motivated to take challenges. Similarly, a CEO of a company can unleash the creative energies of his employees to develop innovative products and services which would have the potential to change industries.

A leader needs to believe in other people that they are capable of doing much more than their present self. This belief, if strong, would be channeled to those who would start to believe in their inherent strength. A leader needs to consistently motivate them by reinforcing this belief and supporting them in their achievements. If we are able to bring the best out of others and drive them to do something constructive, we automatically become a leader.

45: A PERSON SHOULD FEEL GREAT WITH YOU

We keep meeting a large number of people in our life, most of which we forget but some of them we remember always. We would even want to be with them again. We remember a unique charisma these people used to have which made us feel great, even the way we never felt before. These people use to bring so much of optimism in life that we can feel that still now. While these people were full of energy and enthusiasm, we never felt inferior in front of them.

Now, if we look at the above paragraph from a different perspective and become a person who creates an impression which lasts for a lifetime, then how would our life change? If we analyze today's world and the successful people in it then a common aspect which is present in all achievers is that they are able to connect well with others while creating a lasting impression on the people they meet. This means that the said skill is an important factor to get success in life.

If we are clear about the secret of success which is to create a lasting impression on others we meet, then the question arises, how can we do that? The answer to this question may be simple but it requires a lot of practice and fundamental changes in us to use it. For most of the people the central theme of their communication is 'themselves', which is extremely interesting for them but boring for others. People can talk a whole lot of things about themselves ranging from their greatness at work to the problems of their lives to their daily routine. We need to understand that this communication would never leave a good lasting impression on others about you.

If you can make a person feel great with you then you have got the key to make people like you. Humans are emotional creatures and most of their decisions are the result of their emotional intensity for something. If you can connect with them emotionally then they would feel great with you. Three rules need to be followed to achieve this:

- You need to genuinely feel good with them and like them, as without it all of your efforts would look superficial.
- The focus of the communication should be never 'you' i.e. you should not talk about yourself.
- Your focus of communication should be the person you are talking. It means that the communication should rotate around understanding them by listening them, genuinely.

46: DO EVERY TASK SINCERELY

Success is a beautiful, everyone wants it. People may have different definition of success, as for some spending more time with family is success, for others getting healthier is success, for some getting more knowledge is success while for many others earning more money is success. Success for a person is something which gives her happiness and makes her feel complete. If we look around, we would see people who have not much clarity about their definition of success as they are too busy to catch up with others in the race of economic achievements. But once guided properly they can define what success means for them. It is amazing to know the various definitions of success.

It is required to understand that not all of the people are able to get the success they desire. It may have to do with the choices they made and risks they took and the efforts they had put to it. Another important point which differentiates between successful and unsuccessful people is their sincerity for the work they do. Sincerity has various levels and the lowest of which is casualness. Sincerity requires focus and efforts and even if we are proficient in a job, we need to put extra efforts to be among the best. Most people, sadly, over a period of time lose sincerity in the job they do.

It is to be noted that like many other successful people we all cannot be uniquely talented or take high risks in life. Most of us are normal people who may not have any special talent or cannot take high risks to get success. But we all can be always sincere in the tasks we undertake, decisions we take, commitments we make and jobs we do. We should not take anything casually. This minor change in life would be enough to take you to your success.

47: POWER OF PATIENCE CREATE DIFFERENTIATION

Over the last few decades, the life has become extremely fast. All are running to catch up with their peers and to get ahead of them. People are struggling to manage and balance their personal and professional life as they feel that they are losing the control on both. People want to have instant gratification whether it is a dress, food, product or something else. This phenomenon is known as the modern lifestyle in which people do not have the time to think but want everything which someone else has. Modern lifestyle is connected to the emotions of the people which develop pressure in mind. This pressure is the main reason for stress in life which is the beginning of many diseases. In short, this lifestyle affects our emotional well-being, while sucking the happiness out of our life.

It is true that if we are living in 21st century we cannot avoid all these desires and cannot live a life of saints. And, nobody is suggesting that. The only purpose of this point is to know that whatever we do our health and happiness must never be affected negatively; instead, it should grow in the process. The best solution is the simplest one, which is to have patience.

There is nothing bad in the modern lifestyle, only that we have neglected our important ally, which supports us in fulfilling our desires while keeping us sane. It helps us in enjoying every day in our lives while keeping us healthy. It reduces the probability of any disease affecting us. We should embrace our ally by not reacting to the events in life by having patience.

Patience takes rashness from our lives and brings control to it. It adds quality to our decisions and effectiveness to our actions. It helps to correct our mistakes and learn from them. Patience let us enjoy the precious things we have in our lives but were neglected. It also helps us to aim higher and supports in achieving our goals. Some people have a wrong notion that dynamism is opposite of patience, which is not true. In fact, patience is necessary for dynamism, which allows people to have results through efficiency and effectiveness.

It is the choice of the individual to have patience in their life or not. It does not require a lot of efforts, only a simple decision would do. Every person can design their own methods to include patience in their lives.

48: PUNCTUALITY

We keep meeting a lot of people in our life in personal and professional interactions. Some of who gives us soothing feeling while others simply pass-by without having any noticeable impact on us. Though both of these types of people are not much different in looks, communication and behavior but there is certain differentiation which makes them unique. To analyze this fact, we need to understand the most precious asset available to us, which is limited in quantity and diminishes consistently, is time. It is ironical to know that most of the people do not understand the value of time they have in their life. As it is the limited resource and is reducing every minute, we need to utilize it to gain the maximum value out of it.

To utilize time, we need to appreciate it honestly and the first step in this respect is punctuality, which ensures the saving of precious time in your life and others. In many cases any disrespect for time wastes others time too. For example, the delay in meeting wastes our time in addition to the people accompanying us and the people waiting for us, thereby compounding its effect. Punctuality respects time while saving us from unnecessary stress, confusion and conflict. It boosts our confidence and strengthens our self-esteem. It enhances our reputation and respect in the minds of people.

When we meet people who have punctuality and discipline, we tend to feel good about them. They seem to be principled people who are easily liked and can be trusted. We respect them as they respect us and our time, this is the first impression they make on us. Punctuality brings immediate benefits in our life.

Punctuality is the subset of discipline and arises from recognizing the value of the time in our lives. We need to be productive, which indicates that more time would mean more output and results. We need to decide to work at the high-performance levels making us to give time the respect it deserves.

49: RESPECT YOUR WORDS

If we analyze the great feats achieved in the world, we would always find a group of people working together to achieve it. People can perform great things in teams while an individual has his limitations. A team is generally more than the sum of its individual parts as everyone supports each other and weaknesses of a team member is balanced with the strengths of others. Co-ordination and mutual support is the basic requirement of building high performance teams as the lack of these components would make it weak and prone to conflicts and friction.

Trust among team members is of paramount importance to rely on each other which is the necessary aspect of the coordinated actions. A team without trust is unable to perform anything and would break. Trust building is the fundamental element which builds and sustain relationships. A separate book is required to discuss the concept of trust in depth. But if a person wants to become a trustworthy person the easiest way is to start respecting his words. A person who respects his words and keep them can earn the trust of people. It means that we need to speak what we really mean and we would stick to it, otherwise it should not be spoken.

In present times, most of the people speak the words just for speaking. They never intend to mean them or to implement them. These words were spoken to bypass the immediate crises or problem. As they were never serious about their words, they hope same for others, but that is not the case as most people do care about the words which were spoken to them. Unfulfilled promises and hollow words will never allow a genuine relationship to start. And, relationships are very important in every aspect of success in our lives.

If we could start to respect our words by being more careful when speaking them, the life could change for better. To become a trustworthy person, we first need to trust our words. We should speak only those things which we intend to do, otherwise those should not be uttered. In some rare cases if we are not able to do some specific thing for which we agreed, then it should be clarified with the people who could be waiting for it.

50:
PERSEVERANCE

Almost all humans are same, in abilities, in capacities and in intellect. Talent is the unique ability to do something specific better than others. Talent is not gifted but it is developed over time through intent, focus, hard-work and consistency. Deficiency of any of these elements would be resistive in developing any ability.

We all have our own definition of success, which is achieving something specific in our lives. This could be health, money, position, time, power or something else. Whatever it is, genuine efforts would be required to get it. Somehow, such a simple formula is not properly implemented by many people as we do not tend to see lot of successful people. What is the difference between the people who got success and who did not? The answer is perseverance.

Perseverance is the commitment to follow through, even in the face of difficulties and failures. Perseverance aims at the goal and drives a person to it. This simple act would segregate the winners from losers. Perseverance should become the part of nature. The more we persevere the better we become at perseverance.

US President Barak Obama has always stressed upon his ability to persevere as the main reason for his success, same goes for other top entrepreneurs and professionals. Perseverance requires will power which acts as the foundation to move on even if the going is tough, making most others to leave. It provides necessary energy and optimism to endeavor.

About Author

Anshuman is an author and knowledge creator who has transformed the lives and work of people from every continent. His groundbreaking ideas in Thinking, Communication, Personality and Storytelling are revolutionary, simple and effective.

His belief in simplicity has created powerful solutions that can be used by everyone effortlessly.

Experience the free material from following links:

https://direct.me/anshuman

www.ingramcontent.com/pod-product-compliance
Lightning Source LLC
Chambersburg PA
CBHW031305130726
47988CB00007B/2738